water/tongue

water / tongue

mai c. doan

OMNIDAWN PUBLISHING
OAKLAND, CALIFORNA
2019

Cover art: *Water Walker* by Khoa Le, watercolor and digital paint.

Cover & interior typeface: Perpetua Std

Cover & interior design by Cassandra Smith

Offset printed in the United States
by Sheridan, Chelsea, Michigan
On 55# Glatfelter B19 Antique
Acid Free Archival Quality Recycled Paper

Library of Congress Cataloging-in-Publication Data

Names: Doan, Mai C., 1986- author.
Title: Water/tongue / Mai C. Doan.
Description: Oakland, California : Omnidawn Publishing, 2019.
Identifiers: LCCN 2018040171 | ISBN 9781632430656 (pbk. : alk. paper)
Classification: LCC PS3604.O175 A6 2019 | DDC 811/.6--dc23
LC record available at https://lccn.loc.gov/2018040171
Library of Congress Cataloging-in-Publication Data

Published by Omnidawn Publishing, Oakland, California
www.omnidawn.com (510) 237-5472 (800) 792-4957
10 9 8 7 6 5 4 3 2 1
ISBN: 978-1-63243-065-6

PART 1 : DUST

The ordinary response to atrocities is to banish them from consciousness. Certain violations of the social compact are too terrible to utter aloud: this is the meaning of the word unspeakable. Too often secrecy prevails, and the story of the traumatic event surfaces not as a verbal narrative but as a symptom.

if i could go back

happy

1951

birthday

1965

a black hole

1975

treading in the water

1986

a short span of light speeding

[   ]

through a dark dark tunnel

2011

embryonic dream state

2013

soaked in your terror

i wouldn't

I.

THE EARTH AWOKE: hot metal smoking. grazing horses, spilt blood. peanut plants blackened with shock. a normal day: lethal.

SYMPTOMS: evidence of what mouths have refused to say

what is at the root of a body that eats its own lungs?

multi-dimensional terror

YOU WERE NOT ALONE.
YOU HAD BECOME MORE THAN ONE BODY.

II.

here is the house. here is the kitchen. here are the orange trees
that just bloom and bloom and burst. on top of the house, a crack.
where the rain wilts through.

here is the bathtub.
not the first.

hair tangled in the drain.
hair keeps falling out.

4:00 am:

i sweep. and sweep. and sweep. and sweep.

until the dead is swept up
off the floor.

i sweep and sweep and sweep.

until the dead is swept up
and the dead is not
dead anymore.

<u>4:30 am:</u>

i make a tiny dirty body.
i make a tiny dirty body from all
that is left behind from
all that falls off from
all that falls off and gets left
behind.

i sleep in this tiny dirty body.
i blow into it and watch it fly.

tiny ashes.

tiny stars.

tiny dust settles

and sticks to tiny walls.

III.

knife sharp. kitchens aren't made for. little girl, run.
around the block, get the fuck out

of there. is right here. in right hip. in right knee. in right   shoulder.
in stomach and throat: can't run around the block.

suffocate in the cloud
of Marlboro Reds
air puddles dead
at the feet

look down

smash your own
throat shut

little

get out
of the
girl

shake the dead
off your feet.

REMEMBER WHEN [society, bed luck, costumes, lock of family ties, life situations, lock of opportunities, ignorance, lock of medical attention, way of life, most of all family ties, bad choices, lack of medical care] DIED?

REMEMBER WHEN [society, bed luck, costumes, lock of family ties, life situations, lock of opportunities, ignorance, lock of medical attention, way of life, most of all family ties, bad choices, lack of medical care] WENT MISSING?

REMEMBER WHEN [society, bed luck, costumes, lock of family ties, life situations, lock of opportunities, ignorance, lock of medical attention, way of life, most of all family ties, bad choices, lack of medical care] NEVER RETURNED?

REMEMBER WHEN [society, bed luck, costumes, lock of family ties, life situations, lock of opportunities, ignorance, lock of medical attention, way of life, most of all family ties, bad choices, lack of medical care] GOT FOREVER SICK?

REMEMBER WHEN [society, bed luck, costumes, lock of family ties, life situations, lock of opportunities, ignorance, lock of medical attention, way of life, most of all family ties, bad choices, lack of medical care] STOPPED EATING?

i didn't want to be left alone overnight in the hospital with X
i didn't want to be left alone
i didn't want to be left

in the hospital

the nurse changed the bedpan
i changed the bedpan

X was talking to people that weren't there

i had to translate for X to the doctor
i had to translate to the doctor

i couldn't

in the hospital

i started playing candy
crush

in the hospital

X was under the care of
the state

UNDER STAFF OVER FLORESCENCED
JAW LOCK AROUND A PEN
SEIZURE
JUICE BOX
COMA

X was under the care of the state
because

X was under the care of the state
because

X was under the care of the state
because

X was under the care of the state
because

the pills didn't work.

why didn't the pills work?
the first thing X asks after waking up.

                                        X was under the care of the state
                                                                 because

                                        X was under the care of the state

                                                      and the state almost
                                                            killed X again.

IV.

the dead are more alive than the living and i want to know why.

PART 2: WATER/TONGUE

thick

between

hum and prayer

i lie

a tiny radius

of someone else's quiet

slicing through

my own

sound

I.

if i speak if i articulate this new American body into new
American parts if i articulate if i name if i name myself using
correct American words if i articulate this non-American
suffering this non-American pain give it an non-American origin
traceable to a person or place or part of my non-American blood
line or body if i name this non-American suffering make it up
make it about my symptoms not American history about my
symptoms in this non-American flesh but no deeper no darker but
no bigger but no further back i become an American narrative i
become a treatable American narrative i become state-sponsored i
become an American narrative

if i speak if i articulate this new body into new parts if i articulate
if i name if i name myself using correct words if i articulate this
suffering this pain give it an origin traceable to a person or place
or part of my blood line or body if i name this suffering make it
up make it about my symptoms not history about my symptoms
in this flesh but no deeper no darker but no bigger but no further
back i become a narrative i become a treatable narrative i become
state-sponsored i become a narrative

if i speak if i articulate if i articulate if i name if i articulate if i
name i become i become i become

II.

led by the Trưng sisters, women were on the frontlines of

rebellion against 247 years of the first Han Chinese occupation of

Viet Nam. fighting for their freedom and autonomy, in the end

when faced with defeat, drowned themselves in the river.

III.

my great grandmother taught me that love is sometimes survival
and adaptability: when there was no longer a river, she crawled
into the bathtub and bit off her tongue.

she swells her tiny pipe of wind with her black spit her teeth rage against
that misplaced sack her tongue her teeth tiny coated black rage wild on
her tongue her tongue loose her tongue free her teeth bite down tiny rushes
out tiny floods her mouth her tiny wind pipe swells and tiny gushes out
her throat fills with water with flesh her cheeks fill with spit pools like ink
she swells dark blue floats silver her face like

IV.

a history of drowning ourselves in the river:

autonomy or death,
we resist capture.

floating on the surface like a glimmer of

trying to make sense

to choose what story to tell

V.

BEFORE Chinese occupation brought Confucianism
BEFORE French colonialism brought cows
BEFORE U.S empire brought capitalism

I LIGHT A CANDLE IN THE ABSENCE OF HER

BODY AND THEN SHARPEN

MY TEETH

PART 3: EXTRACTIONS

In imagining historical rescue as a one way street, we fail to acknowledge the dependence of the presence on the past. Contemporary critics tend to frame the past as the unique site of need, as if the practice of history were not motivated by a sense of lack in the present.

a beginning,
not an end.

the pull from beyond

the river

a telling

of us

louder than

EXTRACTIONS

THE ENGLISH LANGUAGE

                                        THE STORY

THE TIMELINE

                                        THE LINEAGE

          THE MEMORY CAUGHT IN A FRAME

THE FAMILY

                                        THE FATHER

SPEAKING TO A WHITE-PADDED ROOM

SILENCE, DEAD SILENCE

RITUAL SUFFERING

MILITARY MASCULINITY

MAKE MONEY

MISOGYNY

MASTER SHIVERS

EATING MONEY

                                        NUMBING TEETH

                    FORGETTING NAMES

LOST TONGUE

            SINGULARITY

SIMPLICITY

                            ASSIMLIATION

                                GOOD CREDIT

            BIG EMPTY HOUSE

TATE-SPONSORED SAFE SPACE

MISSING THE VIBRATIONAL PRESSURE POINT

INNOVATIVE EXPLOITATION

HIERARCHICAL HEALING

CALCIFIED CONFERENCES

PROFESSIONALIZED FEELING

NON-PROFIT HUSH

SOCIALIZED SURVEILANCE

THE SELF-POLICING CENTER

OUTRAGE AT A BROKEN WINDOW

CLINGING TO THE STATUS QUO

OCCUPATION AS HAZARD

REPETITIVE STRAIN

REPETITIVE STRAIN

REPETITIVE STRAIN

CRYING OFF THE CLOCK

THE UNITED STATES OF PSYCHIC PROJECTIONS

WRITING ABOUT THE PAST

INTO A WHITE MOUTH

DEATH BY EMOTIONAL LABOR

DEATH BY REPRODUCTIVE LABOR

SPIRITUAL AMNESIA

KARMIC WEATHER PATTERNS

QUIETING THE STORM

it began with listening to my body. witnessing my body. wanting to figure out who and what was living inside of it. it started out as wanting to write about intergenerational trauma and healing as it related to my body and the bodies i have come from. to use my body and the bodies i have come from as sites of information and experiences and symptoms that could reveal or start to talk about the failure, sickness, and cost of the American dream on non-American bodies. even / especially through the violent and uneven processes of assimilation and paths to "success."

after years of writing, articulating, and feeling into the gendered and intergenerational impacts of colonialism, capitalism, patriarchy and American empire for this book, i find there are still things i don't know how say. things i don't know how to say about the women whose stories make up these pages. about myself. about the many ways that colonization has interfered, extracted, and then rooted a dysfunctional system of c/overt values and practices that become enacted through our bodies, families, relationships, and institutions under its presence. from policing and surveillance to patriarchy and productivity. and still: the infinite and unruly ways we thrive. stay wild. stay free.

to write things that have never been verbalized, that have never existed as a verbal recollection, telling, or memory. only as silence. only as physical symptoms. truth is deeper and more multidimensional than what is just said aloud. full of rage and sharpened teeth. i'm not sure what it means to attempt to make a narrative out of pieces that have never been connected outside of my own body. to discipline an ever evolving constellation into something linear and legible. i tried my best to keep my stories free, and yet still to write. to write beyond and in spite of any norms to tell suffering as something weak and digestible.

i couldn't have written this book without ritual. without prayer. without a relationship to the ancestral, the intuitive, the felt. i think of the writing of this book as one long ceremony made up of smaller rituals: a ceremony of healing intergenerational trauma by giving it space to come out of the body. my body. my mother's body. my grandmother's body. my great grandmother's body. each story an opportunity for healing that refuses complicity or assimilation. prayers extracting legacies and systems of violence from the past, present, and future. and in doing so, making room for possibilities more alive and more free.

ACKNOWLEDGMENTS

My deepest love and gratitude to the friends, teachers, and loved ones who have supported me and my poetry along the way: Andrea Abi-Karam, Claudia Leung, Denise Benavides, Francis Mead, Jamal Jones, Jamie Chung, Juliana Spahr, Kenji Liu, Luu Doan, Linda Nguyễn, Mónica Gomery, Phuong Vuong, Sean-Patrick Doan, Stephanie Young, Tessa Micaela Landreau-Grasmuck, and many more: you all are artists and creators of infinite size.

Thank you to the many writers who have inspired my dreaming, feeling, and being in the world in ways that have made me and my poetry more possible: Jackie Wang, Jennifer Tamayo, Leah Lakshmi Piepzna-Samarasinha, M. NourbeSe Philip, Mark Aguhar, Robin D. G. Kelley, Sandra Cisneros, and so many more.

To Jennifer S. Cheng: thank you for making space for me and the possibility of this book. To Rusty Morrison and Omnidawn: thank you for your invaluable insight, support, and most of all, for investing in me and my work. Special thanks to Truong Tran, my kin.

To my past, present, and future ancestors: Thank you for this life and for dreaming and creating (with) me.

To my (blood) family: Thank you for your love.

In love & riot,
mai

NOTES

The quote on page 4 is from *Trauma and Recovery: The Aftermath of Violence - From Domestic Abuse to Political Terror* by Judith Lewis Herman

The quote on page 29 is from *Feeling Backward: Loss and the Politics of Queer History* by Heather Love

Versions of "EXTRACTIONS" have been published in the Asian American Literary Review's *Open in Emergency: A Special Issue on Asian American Mental Health* 2017

mai c doan is a queer, Mexican and Vietnamese writer from Los Angeles, California. She has previously published and performed her work though the National Queer Arts Festival, RADAR Productions, HOLD: a journal, Entropy Magazine, Mixed Up!: A Zine about Mixed Race Queer and Feminist Experience, and more. She is a 2016 recipient of the James D. Phelan Literary Award and holds an MFA from Mills College, where she attended as a Community Engagement Fellow.

water/tongue
mai c. doan

Cover art: *Water Walker* by Khoa Le, watercolor and digital paint.

Cover & interior typeface: Perpetua Std

Cover and interior design by Cassandra Smith

Offset printed in the United States
by Sheridan, Chelsea, Michigan
On 55# Glatfelter B19 Antique
Acid Free Archival Quality Recycled Paper

Publication of this book was made possible in part by gifts from:
Mary Mackey
Francesca Bell
Katherine & John Gravendyk, in honor of Hillary Gravendyk
The New Place Fund

Omnidawn Publishing
Oakland, California
Staff and Volunteers, 2018–2019

Rusty Morrison & Ken Keegan, senior editors & co-publishers
Gillian Olivia Blythe Hamel, senior poetry editor & editor, *Omni Verse*
Trisha Peck, managing editor & program director
Cassandra Smith, poetry editor & book designer
Sharon Zetter, poetry editor and book designer
Liza Flum, poetry editor
Avren Keating, poetry editor & fiction editor
Juliana Paslay, fiction editor
Gail Aronson, fiction editor
SD Sumner, copyeditor
Emily Alexander, marketing manager
Lucy Burns, marketing assistant
Anna Morrison, marketing and editorial assistant
Terry A. Taplin, marketing assistant, social media
Caeden Dudley, editorial production assistant
Hiba Mohammadi, marketing assistant